HOW TO MANIFEST AN AMAZING LIFE

Easily and Effortlessly

Discover How to Become a Conscious Creator and Manifest Your Heart's Desires

By

Diana Yankova

How to Manifest an Amazing Life Easily and Effortlessly

Copyright © 2023 Diana Yankova

All rights reserved. No part of this publication may be reproduced, stored in a retrieval system, distributed, or transmitted in any form or by any means, including photocopying, recording, or other electronic or mechanical methods, without the prior written permission of the publisher, except for the use of brief quotations in a book review.

Disclaimer: The information presented in this publication is the author's opinion and is not intended to be any psychological, professional, health or medical advice. If you need expert assistance, please contact the appropriate professional. The content of this book is for informational and entertainment purposes only and is not intended to diagnose, treat, cure, or prevent any condition or disease. This publication does not replace the advice of a medical professional. Consult your physician regarding any personal health concerns, or before making any changes to your diet or regular health plan. While all attempts have been made to verify the information provided in this publication, the author does not assume any responsibility for errors, omissions, or contrary interpretations of the subject matter. Please note that the author does not make any guarantees about the results of the information shared in this publication. If you use any information from this book, the author assumes no responsibility for your actions.

Table of Contents

INTRODUCTION	5
CHAPTER 1: Realizing Your Superpower	13
CHAPTER 2: Following Your Joy	21
CHAPTER 3: Expanding Your Consciousness	27
CHAPTER 4: Living in the "Now" Moment	33
CHAPTER 5: Practicing Self-Love	43
CHAPTER 6: Raising Your Vibration	55
CHAPTER 7: Using the Law of Attraction	71
CONCLUSION	95
GLOSSARY	97

INTRODUCTION

Something amazing is happening on our planet. We are changing. Our bodies are changing. Our energy is changing. We are being "gently" and sometimes "not so gently" pushed to raise our vibration.

People are "waking up" and discovering incredible truths about the reality we have been living in. Passing the year 2012 allowed for new energies on the planet and a rise in human consciousness. It has to do with the precession of the equinoxes, which refers to an astronomical phenomenon about the motion of the equinoxes along the plane of the orbit of Earth. This is also related to the Galactic Alignment, which is an astronomical term occurring as a result of the precession of the equinoxes. A 26,000-year wobble of the planet, which begins and ends with the sun lining up perfectly with the center of this galaxy, causes this alignment.

On December 21, 2012 the Galactic equator aligned with the solstice point. This has to do with what many people who are "awake" call moving from the third dimension (3D)/third density to the fifth dimension (5D)/fourth density. There is something related to this that you may or may not have experienced. Have you been seeing 11:11 everywhere? Maybe every time you look at the clock it's 11:11 or you notice it somewhere else (license plates, the hour and minute you sent an email, etc.)? Many people on the planet have been experiencing this phenomenon.

Numbers are a universal language. 11 is a master number and it has an important significance of intuition, enlightenment, and insight. The number 11 may represent a start of a spiritual progression. What does it mean when you see 11:11? It signifies illumination. It's a reminder that you already are in the shift described above. The numbers are an awakening code, an activation.

There is a spiritual meaning of 11:11. It's like the Universe knocking on your door and "spirit" winking at you. It tells you that there is more than what you see in the physical world. Humanity and Earth are in the middle of an ascension process. Things are changing. 11:11 is a wake up call related to the planetary awakening of consciousness and a call to oneness.

After you begin seeing 11:11 on your clock, you may start experiencing synchronicities: meeting the right people, being in the right place at the right time, etc. Your consciousness may be starting to expand. 11:11 could also be a specific message for you depending on how much you have progressed on your awakening path. You may be receiving profound messages. Pay attention to what you are thinking and doing when you see the numbers. Are you living in the NOW moment? Are you with anyone? What are they saying? What music is playing? Look at your surroundings. What is happening in your life currently? What insights are coming through?

In addition, 11:11 may mean that your thoughts are manifesting rapidly. If you have been focusing on using the Law of Attraction, make sure that you are only thinking about things that you want to manifest and keep your vibration high all the time.

You might also start seeing other number sequences, such as 111, 222, 333, 444, 9:11, 7:11, 12:12, etc. They are often called "angel numbers" or "spirit numbers" because they may be communicating to you a spiritual message. Each of these number combinations could be trying to tell you something. It's a personal message just for you. For example, if you were thinking of a new idea and you see one of these number combinations, it could be a confirmation that you're on the right track. Listen to your intuition when you see them. Examine what you feel during the first few seconds of noticing the numbers.

If you are not seeing 11:11, maybe you have been seeing other numbers or maybe you haven't been paying attention to numbers. That is ok! If you see 11:11 or another number sequence, take a deep breath, and be grateful that you have seen these numbers. This sends a signal to the Universe to provide more synchronicities and number combinations. You can also ask for a sign of what these numbers mean to you personally.

Seeing 11:11 is just the beginning. You are starting to discover the secrets of the Universe and are embarking on an amazing journey. You will notice that you will start seeing many other numbers. Trust your intuition in each instance that these show up. You may begin learning about what is called "the awakening" (why we are here on Earth and where things are going) and finding the right information at the right time without even looking for it. Next time you see the numbers 11:11, breathe deeply and smile because you know more discoveries are on the way. Enjoy the experience!

What does this have to do with manifesting an amazing life? Since the planet is "ascending," and there are new energies, this is helping people raise their vibration and "clear" low vibrational frequencies, thoughts, beliefs, etc. When we remove the negativity, our life starts to become incredible. Many people are "waking up" and discovering things about reality that we weren't aware of before. Most of us haven't been taught these things in school. Many times we were informed that the opposite is true…and we were even told that all this "stuff" is not possible. We were taught so many things that we "should" be "doing" instead of "being."

I never really liked to "do" many of the things that everyone else was doing. I didn't resonate with a lot of what society told us to do. That's why I lived and worked in four countries, speak four languages, and traveled around the world. I was looking to follow my joy and was able to achieve things that other people only dream of doing. After graduating from one of the top universities in the United States, I worked in marketing for some of the biggest companies in the U.S. and Europe and "created" experiences in my professional and daily life that other people didn't understand how I was able to do them. I followed my joy and did what I wanted to do. In 2014 I started seeing 11:11 and began my spiritual journey and search for answers about reality.

This book will focus on some important topics related to energy, consciousness, frequency, vibration, ascension, and enlightenment, which I have done a lot of research on and practiced in the last few years. This is all fundamental in creating an amazing life. **Many people have written on these subjects, but this book is different because instead of providing complicated explanations of these concepts, it gives you simple methods to manifest things in**

a way that is very easy, fun, and joyful. It will offer you a different perspective than the "traditional" ways we have been "programmed" to live our lives. Each chapter includes easy techniques that you can start using right now to change your life. You can feel into the truth of each topic, and see if it resonates with you. From attracting your heart's desires to changing the weather, this book will show you how to see yourself as the creator inside your creation, manifesting an incredible reality easily and effortlessly!

CHAPTER 1:

Realizing Your Superpower

CHAPTER 1: Realizing Your Superpower

Everyone has a superpower that they may or may not be aware of. You have it too! This is the type of superpower that changes reality and makes your life amazing without you having to "do" much. It has to do with...***your heart***!

The electromagnetic field produced by the heart is many times greater than that produced by the brain. It's not just an organ in the body, but something very powerful that can create miracles in your life. We haven't been taught to use it, but this is where your TRUE power is.

There is a lot of scientific evidence that demonstrates the benefits of having heart and brain coherence. The HeartMath Institute has done a lot of research to scientifically prove this. Scientists, organizations and many other people also have shared a lot of information on how the energy field of the heart works and what happens when we have heart and brain coherence. When we are coherent, our physical, mental, and emotional health improve.

The thing that is really amazing about the heart has to do with what it does to the physical reality around us. When we are in the heart, it makes our energy coherent. When we are coherent, we attract only positive things in our lives.

So how do we get in the heart? One simple technique is to put your hand on your heart and focus your attention on the heart (heart chakra, center of the chest). Some people suggest that you can breathe as if the breath is moving in and out of your heart while you have your attention focused there. This helps you achieve heart and brain coherence.

The HeartMath Institute has free simple techniques that you can also try. They have a free app (the Global Coherence app) that helps you stay coherent by focusing on your breath. You can measure how much coherence you have, so that you know when you have heart and brain coherence. Once you figure out how and when you have it, you can do this without the app during the day. It's very useful to understand when you have this coherence and which techniques help you achieve it. **When you have become aware of how to keep heart and brain coherence, and you are able to maintain this throughout your day, then you will start manifesting amazing things! This is your superpower!**

I have had many incredible experiences with this. The thing that made me very amazed was how I can change the weather by going in the heart. When there was a storm, wind, rain, etc. I just put my hand on my heart, focused my attention there, and started breathing while keeping my awareness on the area around the heart (sometimes a little bit above it because there is also the thymus gland above the heart, which is a very important energy center.). After a few minutes of doing this, the wind/rain slowed down. Then it even stopped! I did this many times. One day when it was raining outside, I decided to listen to a "spiritual" show with people who are "awake" and in the heart. Since both of the speakers were in the heart, as I started listening to them, the energy coming from their voices/sound started to change the way it was raining outside, after which the rain completely stopped! You can try noticing what happens to the weather when you are in the heart and your energy is coherent. **Everything is energy, and your heart is a very powerful energy center that can change your reality and create miracles!**

I also realized that there is another easy way to stay in the heart and have heart and brain coherence. This way is to follow your joy and do the things that you would enjoy doing each moment. Then, you are fully present in your body, not thinking, and are focused on what you are doing (pretty much you are following your heart's desires and you are in the heart). For example, when you are eating something that you enjoy, you are probably having heart and brain coherence in that moment. A great way to check this is to use HeartMath Institute's free Global Coherence app while you are doing different things to see when you are coherent and when you are not. Then you will know when you are using your superpower and when you are not.

"Your heart can change your reality and create miracles!"

@choosamazing

Your head can plant in your nails!
And create cupcakes!

@chocoseaarch

CHAPTER 2:

Following Your Joy

CHAPTER 2: Following Your Joy

One way to have an amazing life and heart and brain coherence is to follow your joy and excitement. This means that in any given moment you can feel (not think, but FEEL) what activity makes you the most excited and do that. Apply this strategy throughout the day for everything: chores, work, relationships, choices, etc.

If doing something makes you feel good, then you are following the guidance of your authentic self (Higher Self/true self) and intuition. Become aware of how you feel when you are about to make a choice. Before you do anything, check in with your feelings. If you do things that don't make you happy, then you are not listening to your authentic self.

When I talk about following your joy, this means things that actually produce "real" joy. It doesn't mean doing anything to harm anyone else. Some people might think they feel "good" doing something to hurt someone, but this is not "joy" and this is NOT what I am referring to in this chapter. I am talking about REAL joy (which is listening to your heart and intuition without harming anyone).

It's important to be in the NOW moment. When you get distracted, then you might not notice what your body is telling you. If you have to perform something that you don't enjoy doing, wait until a later time when you may feel better about it. For example, if you have to do chores and you don't have any excitement about doing that in a particular moment, wait until you start feeling better about that activity. Your energy levels and vibration can increase during the day and you may get an urge to do them at a later time. Follow your joy. If you would rather relax first and then do chores, then this is the order that you can go with.

Pay attention to your emotions and intuition. You will see how you will start attracting fun experiences in your life. By choosing only what feels good, you will be presented with more options that make you happier. You will then enjoy positive emotions, you will stay at a high vibration and experience a higher frequency. This can help you manifest amazing things, even if you don't know what you want!
When you have trouble deciding between two possibilities, choose the one that makes you feel good.

This strategy is absolutely amazing. It lets you live better without much effort (because you will only be doing things that you ENJOY and that bring you EXCITEMENT) without having to specifically decide what you want to manifest. By following what brings you joy and bliss, you will automatically start attracting awesome things into your life.

If you don't believe that it can be this simple to create an incredible life for yourself, then try it out and see how everything can improve. When you start to follow your excitement every moment of each day, there will be amazing changes in your life. You will vibrate higher and experience synchronicity after synchronicity. Life will become magical! Follow your joy!

"By choosing what brings you joy, you will be presented with more options that make you happy."

@choosamazing

CHAPTER 3:

Expanding Your Consciousness

CHAPTER 3: Expanding Your Consciousness

Consciousness is awareness. It is being aware of what is happening in the moment. Many spiritual teachings, such as nonduality, say that we are consciousness. There are many practices and techniques to figure out "who" we are, but **it can be as simple as just realizing when you are aware that you are aware**. This is also what nonduality teachers explain is "enlightenment." You simply become pure consciousness (by being aware in the moment). Instead of focusing on the objects, people, and things in your environment, you can focus on awareness.

This awareness has no time/space/limits. When you are aware that you are aware, do you see any limits to this awareness? Spiritual teachers explain that everything is consciousness.

So how is this related to manifesting an amazing life? When you are aware in the moment (instead of being in your thoughts), you can change reality. From my personal experience, I have had many things happen when I wasn't aware in the moment. Even before learning about consciousness, I had noticed that when I was "in my thoughts" and not present in the moment, something not so "pleasant" would happen to get me to get back to the now moment. I was receiving "reminders" to get me out of my thoughts and back to becoming aware of what is happening in the moment.

Quantum physics explains that when we are aware, we can change the outcome of what happens in our reality. There are experiments related to this that demonstrate that the results change based on if there is an observer or not (such as the famous double-slit experiment). This shows the effect that consciousness has on reality.

When you are not aware of what is happening each moment, there can be "interference," which doesn't allow you to experience the highest outcome you can experience in that moment. This is also shown in experiments in quantum physics.

In order to manifest an amazing reality, it is important to be fully present and aware each moment (instead of being lost in your thoughts). When you are in the moment, you are in a different "dimension" than if you are in your thoughts. The thoughts are in a dimension with a lower frequency, so when you put your focus there, your frequency is lower than if you focus on the present moment.

Focus is also very important because energy goes where you put your attention. So if you place your focus on a low frequency "dimension," then you create something that is of a lower vibration. If you put your focus on something that is higher frequency, this will give you a more positive outcome.

Consciousness is fundamental in reality creation. It is important to be aware of what you put your attention on, and to choose those things/places/people that have a high vibration and something that you would like to see manifest in your life. If you are not conscious, and if you put your focus randomly on random things (or on something low vibrational, such as the news or anything else that is negative and creates fear), then what you manifest probably will not be what you would like to experience. You can try to see what happens in your reality when you are aware in the moment and are focusing your attention on something positive, and what happens when you are "in your thoughts."

"Enlightenment is being aware that you are aware."

@choosamazing

CHAPTER 4:

Living in the "Now" Moment

CHAPTER 4: Living in the "Now" Moment

Everyone has heard about how we should live in the "now moment" and "be present," but what does that actually mean? For many people, it is difficult to be in the moment, and they don't understand the benefit. Being in the "now" does a lot more than just help you relax or meditate.

When I was in Ecuador for a spiritual retreat, I had an amazing encounter with the plant medicine San Pedro. I had never tried anything like it before and didn't know what to expect. After doing a lot of research, I discovered that it can help to see beyond the veil of this 3D illusion and to experience oneness (this is related to the planetary ascension and the meaning of 11:11 that I explained earlier). For this reason, I decided to try it.

What happened was extraordinary. I wasn't just "hallucinating" as many skeptics would say. There is a good reason why it is called "plant medicine." It is to be taken for a spiritual purpose and has been used by shamans for so long (I am in no way suggesting that you should do this, this is just my experience).

San Pedro expanded my mind and let me see beyond the illusion of the 3D matrix (the world we have been living in). I was actually able to witness myself as the "creator inside my creation!" I saw that everything around me is like a game in which I am the player/character, along with all of the other people in my life. Everyone has a role, and everything happens for a specific reason. Positive and negative experiences are all perfectly orchestrated by....us! Or more specifically, our authentic self ("Higher Self" / true self). I saw that everything is PERFECT and happens in the perfect moment.

It was absolutely amazing to be able to actually see, feel, and know that every moment of our lives is perfectly designed as part of this life "game." Everything really DOES happen for a reason. I experienced myself outside of the game as the observer or the "one," and at the same time, I was inside the game as the character playing a certain role. I saw and felt the "oneness" and the "allness." The oneness - we are all one, and the allness - we are many different expressions of the one.

So how does living in the moment relate to this? I realized that since everything is already pre-planned/organized and co-created by my authentic self (Higher Self/true self or what some people call Source/the Divine/God, etc.) and I am just here playing this "game," it's important to stay centered and be present every moment of each day. This is because the purpose of the game is to EXPERIENCE and remember our AUTHENTIC SELF. I understood that if you are not fully aware in the moment, you are missing the experience. By living "in the now" instead, you can manifest an incredible life because negative thoughts and emotions don't get in the way.

You are always living in the now. When you are doing something, you are doing it "now." When you are thinking about the past or the future, you are doing it "now." Are you ever doing anything that is not happening "now"? *The "now" is all there is.* The point is to be aware of what happens in your "reality" each moment. You are always "aware," so you just need to become aware that you are aware. This is also what I stated in the previous chapter that spiritual teachers call "enlightenment." I learned that it is just being aware that you are aware because everything is about consciousness. It sounds too simple, but if you have read or watched anything about nonduality, this is how enlightenment is explained. However, the physical body also has to clear the low vibrational frequencies/emotions, which is a part of the "enlightenment/ascension" process.

After the profound experience I had with San Pedro, I started to practice being present as much as possible during each day. I noticed that I wasn't thinking as much (which is usually so difficult to NOT do!). When I do this, I experience such peace and harmony in everything that happens to me during the day. I don't have to plan what I am going to do next because I get "downloads," intuitive knowings or amazing ideas, which I never would have thought of otherwise. When I am present in the NOW moment, my thoughts stop and I just feel so peaceful. The day flows, experiences flow, everything flows.

    When you observe your "now moment," you might not perceive things that happen as problems because you know that they are simply part of the game of life. You realize that everything means something that will lead to an important experience (which in this "pre-planned or Higher Self/Source/Divine co-creative game" is going to happen anyway, so why worry, since YOU designed it that way!?).

    By being in the present moment, you feel good and there isn't really a need to try to manifest anything using the Law of Attraction because you automatically attract what is for your highest good. Miracles happen! They come to you, instead of struggling and trying to "do" something to make things or people appear. Everything is in perfect flow and you are presented with the right situations for you to experience. You still take action, but it is inspired and based on following your joy and excitement.

Your consciousness expands, your vibration raises, and your life just gets more and more magical.

Here is a living in the "now" technique: All you have to do to "live in the now" is to observe each moment, become aware that you are aware, and ACCEPT everything that happens to you, with you or around you as being absolutely perfect and part of the game. Be grateful for every single experience, whether positive or negative. Completely SURRENDER to each moment. TRUST that all is well, exactly as it should be and is happening for your benefit. KNOW that everything will work out.

There is a specific reason for every occurrence, and there are no "coincidences." What we experience depends on our frequency, vibration, and if we are aware in the moment or not. So if we are not aware and are not high frequency, in order to experience a reality that we will enjoy, it's useful to find a way to stay out of thoughts, be aware, and do something that feels good or access a feeling state that is high frequency (love, gratitude, joy, peace, etc.).

Accepting what is happening also helps to raise your vibration. For instance, even if a dish falls and breaks, just say to yourself that this is perfect and you accept the experience. When you start practicing this strategy regularly for EVERYTHING in EVERY instance, "negative" experiences will go away. By centering yourself, taking deep breaths, and focusing on your surroundings and on what you are doing each moment, your thinking will slowly calm down until you reach a point of having no thoughts (yes, it is actually possible!). You will get to a place of neutrality and what's called the "zero point."

Reality creation is a much deeper subject having to do with what is "pre-destined" and what we create as we go. Being aware of the present moment is a good place to start exploring this and discover what YOUR truth is.

From the very start of your day just be the observer of yourself in your environment, knowing that you are a character in this "game" or "play." For example, you can notice: "now I get up; now I am brushing my teeth; my breakfast is delicious," etc. Pay attention to everything that is happening. Just OBSERVE yourself as a character in a game. Be the "creator inside your creation" and see how your life will improve. Things will easily come to you without you having to think about or plan anything!

**"You are always living in the "now."
The "now" is all there is."**

@choosamazing

CHAPTER 5:

Practicing Self-Love

CHAPTER 5

Practicing Self-Love

CHAPTER 5: Practicing Self-Love

What is self-love and why is it important for everyone to love themselves? What if you don't like the way you look or some of your habits? How can you truly love yourself and how does that affect your daily experience? I present to you what I believe self-love is and how it creates your reality. Take a deep breath and feel if this resonates with you.

Let's look at what loving yourself really means. There are many strategies listed by spiritual teachers and "experts," such as looking at yourself in the mirror every day and telling yourself "I love you" (or at least start with "I like you" until you can believe the first phrase). There is also another angle to how you can approach the issue of self-love. Every person already IS love. At the core of our being is love and light. It has just been clouded by fear, anger, anxiety, and other negative emotions and limiting beliefs. Think of this like the layers of an onion. When you peel the layers, you get to the core, which in this case is love. So in order to love oneself, it means to peel all the unnecessary limiting layers and be your authentic self 100% of the time!

By being YOU, you ARE being LOVE! By being PRESENT and aware in the moment, you are being love. Self-love can be as easy and as simple as observing yourself in the moment ("living in the now"). What are you doing? What are you thinking? What is appearing around you? When you are present and aware, you are your TRUE SELF, which is LOVE.

Also, by being true to who you are, you are practicing self-love. That means to always be yourself and to only do things that align with your true desires. Don't do anything you don't want to do, don't say anything that you don't mean, and don't be involved with anything not true to yourself.

For example, let's say that someone asks you to go somewhere with them. If you don't want to, don't go. If you decide to go to be "polite," then you're not being true to yourself and are not respecting yourself. You need to learn to say no. This doesn't mean that you should be rude to others, not at all. You can politely decline an invitation.

The point here is that if you do things that you don't want to do, then you're not loving yourself. Being authentic, being yourself, means to follow your joy and excitement all the time, every second of the day. If something doesn't make you happy, don't do it. If you do things for others out of obligation, then that goes against being true to your wants and desires and is not self-love. If it doesn't make you feel good, it's probably not something that you should be involved in.

Doing only things for yourself that make you happy is not selfish. It can actually be service to others! Being selfish is when you lie or manipulate others for your personal benefit. The actions of lying and manipulating are not coming from love, therefore they're not from your true self. So, if you try to manipulate someone or do something that hurts or deceives them, then you are not practicing self-love. If you accept something that you actually don't want to accept, what do you think that means? If you do things that don't bring you joy, just to please others, is that being real with others?

By staying true to what you want or don't want, you are in fact helping people by showing them what they need to see or hear to assist them to realize what negative beliefs they may have about themselves and their lives. For example, let's say a friend asks you to go to the movies and you decline because you don't want to go. Your friend might then complain about how no one likes them. This situation can help this person become aware of the fact that they have limiting beliefs about themselves. If you had not declined the invitation, would your friend have realized this? If he didn't have any negative beliefs, he wouldn't have reacted that way. By understanding what is lurking in his subconscious mind, this person can work on releasing any negative thoughts and emotions.

Loving yourself also means to stop judging yourself, whether that would be your physical appearance, your actions, your experiences, or what you did or didn't do in the past. Don't judge yourself. Forgive yourself for EVERYTHING. Every single thing. Forgiving yourself raises your vibration and you automatically start changing your reality.

So how can you forgive yourself? Have compassion for yourself. For many people this may sound like a difficult thing. A way to do this is to realize that every event that happened in your life was designed to help your evolution in some way. The actions that you are judging yourself for had a purpose. The things that others did to you had a purpose. Look at life like a game. Every character has a role to play and they (and YOU) played it perfectly.

If there is an area in your life that you're not happy with, it's trying to show you where you're not loving yourself. Let's dive deeper into this. Your external reality reflects your internal state. If you have limiting beliefs, fears, doubt, anger, negative thoughts, etc., then what happens around you will demonstrate that. For example, if you are afraid of something, you will attract it in your environment to SHOW you that you have fear related to that specific thing. If someone makes you angry by taking a certain action, this helps you REALIZE that you hold some negative beliefs regarding that action. You might have been unaware of this subconscious belief until this person made you aware of it by causing you to get angry. If this hadn't happened, how would you have known? Do you see the benefits and the GIFT of the situation? Instead of judging this person and blaming them for what they did, look at what you GAINED from this experience. You are a mirror for others and they are a mirror for you.

If someone made you feel less than, tried to take advantage of you, or did anything else to dim your light, it's because they saw something in you that you didn't see in yourself...they realized how AMAZING you are and felt threatened by it! For example, if a colleague at work tried to get you fired or said something to make you look bad in front of others, it's because they were jealous of what you had and what you were capable of. Even if you didn't know your worth, they sure noticed how worthy you are! Otherwise, why would they go through all the trouble of manipulating, doing things behind your back and trying to make you look bad? It's because they knew you were so GOOD at what you did, whether you realized it or not. Or maybe you are also very attractive and they were jealous of you (maybe you don't realize how attractive you are). When we look at this situation from a higher perspective, we will see the benefits.

This person was actually assisting you to realize your worth and trying to get you to be your authentic self. If you didn't like your job, they helped you discover that there is something more amazing for you to do in life and that you should quit. They did you an enormous favor! So instead of feeling bad about how they lied and tried to steal your light, view this scenario as an awesome experience that allowed you to see how magnificent you actually are. All of this was designed to help you love yourself.

When you apply this strategy to everything that occurred in your life, you will see the lessons and gifts of everything that you experienced. This can help you have compassion and forgive yourself for EVERYTHING. Your life has a purpose and your soul and authentic self ("Higher Self") is guiding you every step of the way. Trust yourself!

You've probably heard people say "everything happens for a reason" and it actually does! There is a reason you were born on a specific date, in a particular place to your parents, and with the name that you were given. These are no accidents. There are NO coincidences. Everything has a purpose. When you realize this, you can let go of any resentments and forgive yourself and others. Every situation, every conversation, every experience has a specific purpose. Maybe you were meant to make someone aware of something. Maybe they were meant to teach you something.

Don't feel guilty or resentful. These negative emotions only lower your vibrational frequency and make you attract negative experiences into your life. Forgiving yourself does the opposite. It increases your vibration and helps you attract positive things. This of course has to do with the Law of Attraction.

Remember that what is on the inside is what is reflected on the outside. Hence, how you feel about yourself is directly related to what you experience in your life. If you can't forgive yourself and if you don't love yourself, then you attract events, people, and situations that match that. For example, if you (consciously or subconsciously) judge yourself about the foods that you eat, then you might manifest someone who will criticize you about your eating habits, thus showing you YOUR inner critic about the issue! The value of that situation would be to make you aware of this self-criticism. You can avoid having to experience such a situation by just forgiving yourself and being authentic. Then you can attract people who will be kind and supportive. Do you see how this works?

When you love everything about yourself, when you are BEING authentic, you have a high vibration and attract incredible things/people/situations in your life. Everything starts working out like magic!This is not just some "woo woo" theory, it's 100% true.

You are amazing. You are worthy. You ARE love! You are a Divine being. YOU are the miracle! If anyone told you otherwise, they were just helping you (consciously or subconsciously) to remember this truth.

Loving yourself means being fully present in the moment, being true to who you are, not judging yourself, and forgiving yourself for everything. Be authentic. Be 100% YOU! This is practicing self-love, which then attracts positive experiences into your life and creates a reality that you can enjoy every day.

"By being YOU, you ARE being LOVE!"

@choosamazing

CHAPTER 6:

Raising Your Vibration

CHAPTER 6: Raising Your Vibration

Everything around us is energy. What you attract into your life depends on the vibrations that you are emitting. Just like with a radio, if you want to listen to a specific radio station, you must select it. You have to "tune in" to the frequency that you would like to experience. Therefore, it is extremely important to keep a high vibration all the time (if you want to attract positive experiences).

There is no good/bad and right/wrong (this is all judgment and duality). However, you probably prefer (preference is different from judgment) some experiences more than others (which I refer to in this book as "positive" and "negative" experiences). There shouldn't be judgment about what is happening with anyone or anything in your life (judgment only lowers your frequency). The thing that you CAN do to change something that you don't prefer is to raise your vibration.

Yes, it is possible to feel good nonstop. If you are familiar with the Law of Attraction, then you know how essential raising your vibration is when you are in the process of manifesting what you want quickly. If your vibration is low, then it is very likely that you will have negative experiences. You are a powerful creator! You attract things into your life every minute of every day.

You create your reality. The energetic vibration that you have determines what you will bring into your daily experience. Your vibration in the current moment attracts more of that same vibration. Therefore, it is absolutely crucial that you keep your vibration high.

So how can you raise your vibration to manifest your heart's desires or simply to feel good and experience a higher frequency?

1. **Set an intention for what you would like to create each day.** Begin every morning by setting positive intentions. Take a deep breath, smile, and confidently say the statement "I KNOW today is going to be an amazing day" or something similar. The phrase "I know" is very powerful and creates more certainty in your feelings than if you just said "Today is going to be an amazing day." The second phrase can work too, but the first one can be perceived as more believable.

2. **Remove what doesn't serve your highest good.** Sometimes raising your vibration is as simple as removing anything that lowers it. Move away from negative people and situations. Stop

watching the news. Don't watch TV or movies that contain any types of scenes, images, or sounds that can make you experience negative emotions. Without realizing it, you may be exposed to subliminal messages and other effects that can impact your energy levels and implant negative ideas in your subconscious mind.

3. **Focus on your heart.** Put a hand on your heart/heart chakra. The electromagnetic field of the heart is much greater than that of the brain. There are many techniques on achieving heart and brain coherence, which is very beneficial for your frequency and your physical body. When you focus your attention on your heart, it raises your vibration and can change your reality!

4. **Try energy healing.** Listen to energy healing mp3s, audio/video, or get energy work sessions from an energy practitioner to remove any low vibrational frequencies from your body and energy field. This can provide a permanent increase in your frequency.

5. **Change your perspective.** Our perception changes reality. By choosing to see the gift and positivity in everything, our vibration goes up.

When we change the way we view a situation, we change the energy and raise our frequency.

6. **Do something that makes you feel good and creative.** Do you have any hobbies? Take your attention off of anything that may be lowering your vibration and focus it on what you enjoy doing. Always remember: where attention goes, energy flows! Creating something new gets your right brain involved. When you use your creativity, you feel good and vibrate higher!

7. **Be grateful.** List out loud or write down at least 5 things that you are thankful for in that moment. Your health, your family, your friends, your accomplishments, something that is abundant in your life, etc.

8. **Feel the emotion of love.** The feeling of love is said to be of the highest frequency. When you live in the love vibration, your frequency is high! This lifts you to a higher state of consciousness. It is an amazing vibration to experience in order to manifest positive things into your life and will help tremendously when using the Law of Attraction. If you're having trouble feeling the emotion of love, you could try remembering how you feel about a

pet or a family member that you love. Stop what you are doing, focus, and send love to them.

9. **Meditate.** There are so many different types of guided meditations available for free online. Do a sitting or walking meditation, focus on your energy centers, such as your heart, or try one that resonates with you. You can also just simply straighten your spine and concentrate on your breath. Inhale deeply and take a longer time on the exhale.

10. **Laugh or watch someone who is laughing.** It sounds simple, but it works. Next time you think to yourself "How do I raise my vibration?" just look at someone laughing!

11. **Dismiss negative thoughts.** Speaking of laughing…next time you notice any negative thoughts, dismiss them by laughing at them. Say to yourself that these negative thoughts are not yours and just laugh. You need to be conscious of your thoughts every moment of the day and dismiss any negativity as soon as it comes. Tell yourself that you are not your thoughts and that your mind is your servant.

12. **Look at life like a game.** If you have to do something that you don't enjoy, such as buying groceries or doing chores, turn it into a game. What would a child do in your place? How would they play? Take a different approach to situations that would normally be considered boring or annoying.

13. **Become aware of the present moment.** Say out loud "I AM Present" or "I AM here." Look at your hands, your body, and your surroundings. Know that everything is OK in that instant. You don't have to think about the past or future. Take a deep breath and simply BE present.

14. **Move your body.** Dancing or just doing any type of movement with your arms and legs can energize you and change your vibration. Smiling while dancing around will make a difference in how you feel. Try it and you will see. Dancing releases endorphins and lifts your mood. You can also try stretching, walking, exercising, swimming, yoga, tai chi, or anything else that resonates with you. Or just jump up and down and excite the cells in your body. Get moving and your energy and vibration will rise.

15. **Go out in nature.** Walking barefoot on grass or sand or taking a swim can be very energetically cleansing, grounding and uplifting. See the beauty of nature and experience the oneness with everything around you. Gazing at the sun at sunrise and sunset can also increase your vibration and help expand your consciousness (the sun is very powerful in many ways).

16. **Use essential oils.** Uplift your mood and change your vibrational frequencies with scents, such as orange, lemon, jasmine or any other of your favorite essential oils.

17. **Shift your vibration with food.** Be mindful of your diet. Avoid low vibrational meals. Eating fruits and vegetables should help increase your vibration. Raw, organic and unprocessed food has a higher vibration. Drinking plenty of water throughout the day helps to flush out toxins from your body. In addition, avoiding alcohol, meat, and chemically altered foods can help your body experience a higher vibration. Notice your energy levels after eating certain foods. Do you feel tired or energized? Paying attention to this will help you determine which foods are raising your vibration and which are lowering it. You are what you eat,

so if you're wondering how to increase your vibration, this is something to try.

18. **Change the vibration of your water.** Shift the frequency of the water that you drink by charging it with the frequency of love. Dr. Masaru Emoto has demonstrated that water can be affected by the energetic frequencies of our words and thoughts. You can change the vibration of your water, and thus vibrate higher yourself. For example, write the word "love" on a piece of paper and put it under your glass of water. The crystalline structure of the water will change, and you will then be drinking the vibrational frequency of love!

19. **Listen to uplifting music.** This can instantly boost your energy, raise your vibration, shift your frequency, and expand your consciousness. Spend time listening to 432 Hz (known for its healing and balancing benefits) or 528 Hz (known as the "miracle tone" and the frequency of love) and see how you feel. In general, Solfeggio frequencies usually have a very positive effect on one's feeling and emotional state. There are many great videos/audios online with music that quickly changes your vibration.

20. **Appreciate something beautiful around you.** Look at your surroundings. There must be something that you find interesting and pleasing to the eyes. If not, then you can search online for images of locations or things that you consider beautiful. Try to start recognizing the beauty in everything.

21. **Daydream.** Visualizing a situation that you desire to be in changes your vibrational alignment. This also helps with the Law of Attraction and makes you aligned with what you want.

22. **Nap.** If you're having trouble shifting your vibrational state, sometimes a good thing to do is to take a nap. When you wake up, your body and mind will be more rested and it should be easier to change your vibration.

23. **Say daily "I am" affirmations out loud with confidence.** You can also do so silently, but saying them out loud boosts the effect. For example, " I AM happy," "I AM a powerful creator," "I AM amazing," "I am prosperous," or any other statement that makes you feel good.

24. **Be nice to someone.** When you make others smile and feel good, you feel good. Compliment a stranger. Tell someone how much you appreciate them. Be mindful of the words you speak because they also carry a vibration. If you say negative things to or about others, your energetic vibration lowers.

25. **Read a high vibe book and/or watch something inspirational.** Reading motivational information and watching people who inspire you can immediately change your vibrational state.

26. **Play with animals.** Animals are pure love and can instantly change how you feel. They teach us unconditional love. If you don't have a pet around you, look at videos or pictures online of your favorite animal.

27. **Surround yourself with people who make you feel good.** Stay away from those who bring you down and spend time with others who are positive and uplifting. You become like the people you hang out with, so choose wisely!

28. **Hug someone.** Hug your pet, your friends, your family members, anyone! Hugging can calm your nervous system and make you feel better.

29. **Do some type of spiritual practice.** No matter what your faith or beliefs, focusing on something spiritual can make you feel better and give you a reason to look beyond your everyday issues. Explore the universe! Ponder your existence. Why do you think you are on this planet? Be curious. Practice spiritual awareness. Searching for the answer within yourself or from outside sources can be a great way to focus on something that can turn out to be pretty fun and exciting.

30. **Clear your fears.** Listen to mp3s that energetically clear negative emotions or work with an energy practitioner to remove any fears and negative energy (visit https://choosamazing.com for free info and tips on the easiest ways to do this). Once you get rid of your fears, you clear unwanted vibrations and make room for positive feelings.

31. **Forgive yourself or another.** Low vibrations are many times caused by not forgiving yourself

or someone else. Forgiving is SO POWERFUL! Forgive and you will immediately remove negative emotions and feel a change in your energy. Feel your vibration raising!

32. **Follow your joy always.** Throughout the day ask yourself what would make you feel the most excited out of all of the options that you have of things to do. For example, if you could choose to either cook, go for a walk, go to the beach, start a project, etc., which of these would give you joy? Select the experiences that make you feel good and follow this strategy all day long. You will be amazed at how much better you will start to feel if you do this all the time.

33. **Burn white sage.** This is a popular way to remove any negative energy from your energy field and your home and environment. Sometimes you can feel an instant boost in how you feel right away. Just let the smoke from the burning sage move around your body to clean anything that may need to be removed. Sage is also a great air disinfectant in addition to its ability to clear negative energy.

34. **See other people as yourself.** If you are talking with someone or are having an issue with someone, imagine them being YOU. How would that change your conversation? Your vibration will most likely go up. You can feel compassion and love speaking with "yourself."

It is important to work on removing any negative emotions and limiting beliefs that you have stored in your subconscious mind. These can pop out of nowhere and lower your vibration at random times, so you should focus on getting rid of any old programming that does not serve you. Paying attention to your thoughts is a good way to start. Then, you can use the solutions mentioned above to experience a quick vibrational shift.

Practice these and you should see a change in your vibration. You CAN feel good all the time. Since you are creating your reality, then it is absolutely necessary to keep a high frequency all day long. The minute that you notice a lowering of your vibration, start laughing, dancing, put a hand on your heart, or do some type of energy practice to instantly increase it. You are powerful. You are a creator. What would you like to create today? Now that you know how to raise your vibrational frequency, make your reality amazing!

"Your perception changes your vibration."

@choosamazing

CHAPTER 7:

Using the Law of Attraction

CHAPTER 7: Using the Law of Attraction

In addition to being in the heart and in the now moment, as well as following your joy, understanding and using the Law of Attraction is another way to create an amazing life. Maybe you would like to manifest money and abundance, a relationship, or something else? You may have tried using the Law of Attraction, which has gained popularity in the last few years with the book and movie *The Secret*. Maybe you have even tried a manifesting course or a manifestation meditation and are still wondering how to make your dreams a reality.

    The Law of Attraction is an amazing tool that you can use to attract what you want and manifest your desires. This refers to manifesting money, love, or anything else in your life. This is not just some "woo woo" idea, but something that is actually based on quantum physics and science. If you search online, you will find specific explanations of how this works and countless Law of Attraction success stories. People apply it to get wealth, win the lottery, attract a specific person, find love, and more. Many use a Law of Attraction planner/journal or a vision board to write their manifestation goals. They visualize the object or outcome they desire and document what they manifest.

So how does the Law of Attraction work? It basically focuses on the idea that like attracts like, meaning that positive thoughts, beliefs and emotions attract positive experiences and negative thoughts, beliefs, and emotions attract negative experiences. So if you have a positive mindset and feel happy, you get positive results. This is the simple explanation, but I will go into more detail below.

Something that many people don't know is that this law is also affected by other universal laws, one of which is the Law of Vibration. It focuses on the fact that everything is always in motion and vibrates at a certain frequency. So what you attract into your life depends on your vibration and frequency. Hence, it is important to raise your vibration and keep it high in order to get what you want. This will make more sense in the following explanation of the importance of feelings when it comes to manifesting anything you want.

Now let's focus on HOW to manifest quickly the things that you would like to have in your life. The tips on this page are the key to using the Law of Attraction to attract what you desire. A theory is one thing, but actual daily practice is what matters. Many people don't know how to use the Law of Attraction correctly to manifest their desires fast. You can "manifest" anything you want. The process for you can be simple or it can be difficult. This depends on your intentions, beliefs, emotions, and actions.

How do you feel right now? Happy? Sad? Something else? If your answer is a positive emotion, you are currently attracting positive things and experiences into your life. If your answer is a negative emotion, then you are attracting negative things. Have you ever wondered why happy people are always "lucky" and get what they want? Or why negative people are always complaining about bad things happening to them? Do you know anyone like that? We attract what we think about, what we believe and what we feel. You have probably heard the phrase that "thoughts become things".

When it comes to using the Law of Attraction, three words are usually the focus: ask, believe, receive. You ASK for what you want, you BELIEVE you can have it, and you wait to RECEIVE it.

Below you will find some tips on how to use the Law of Attraction to bring amazing things into your life. Some of them may seem cheesy or "woo woo," but if you really make the effort and focus, they will work. These tips for manifesting what you desire may sound simple, but they are very powerful and effective when using the Law of Attraction.

The Law of Attraction Manifesting Formula

1. Remove all negative emotions & limiting beliefs from your subconscious mind

2. Set specific intentions & describe in detail what you want to manifest

3. Visualize your goal and believe you already have it

4. Feel positive emotions: love and gratitude

5. Expect to get it and let go

6. Take inspired action

7. Be grateful after you successfully manifest what you want

How to Manifest What You Desire: the Process

1. REPROGRAM YOUR SUBCONSCIOUS MIND AND CLEAR NEGATIVE EMOTIONS

IMPORTANT: Others may not have told you this, but reprogramming your subconscious mind and beliefs is a crucial step to manifesting your dream life and attracting your desires faster. This is something that you must address before you start manifesting. Many Law of Attraction strategies miss this key fact in the manifestation process. You can set an intention and think you believe something and wait to receive it, but if you have subconscious blocks, you won't be successful with the Law of Attraction. Since belief is a crucial part of manifesting, it is necessary to remove any negativity from your subconscious mind that might be limiting your beliefs.

When you decide on a goal that you would like to manifest, carefully examine what you believe about it and how you feel about it. Be honest about your fears. Make a list of the reasons why you might not want your goal to manifest. That should help you become aware of your limiting beliefs. If there are no reasons why you might not want to manifest something, then you most likely have no limiting beliefs. Otherwise, you will have to replace those negative beliefs with positive ones before you can start manifesting your desires.

What you manifest using the Law of Attraction depends on your subconscious programming. Consciously you may want something and you might think that you have a positive attitude toward it, but your subconscious mind may be cluttered with negative beliefs about it. You may think that you believe something, but your subconscious might not agree. If you're not manifesting what you want, you may have to reprogram your subconscious mind and clear any limiting beliefs and negative emotions.

You could have limiting beliefs and blocks that would have to be removed before you can see results. For example, if you can't manifest money, think about what your thoughts are about money. Are they positive or filled with fear and doubt? You will need to analyze your thoughts and feelings about the thing or experience that you are trying to manifest.

If you have any type of resistance (any negative emotions such as fear, doubt, anger, anxiety, guilt, etc.), associated with what you want to manifest, you will probably not have success with the Law of Attraction. **It is very important that you recognize and clear your conscious** *and subconscious limiting beliefs before you start manifesting what you desire.*

TIP 1: Say mentally to yourself the statement that you think you "believe in" and see how that makes you feel. For example: "I believe that I can win $1,000,000 from the lottery." Do you notice butterflies in your stomach, anxiety, or some other weird feeling? If so, you most likely have limiting beliefs and need to reprogram your subconscious mind. How can you become a millionaire if you don't believe that you can?? You HAVE to believe something at the subconscious level in order to manifest it.

TIP 2: Try muscle testing. This interesting technique can reveal very useful insights about your feelings and beliefs that you may not be aware of. You can use it for the same statements that you used for the exercise above. You can search online how to do muscle testing if you haven't tried it.

Once you have identified your limiting beliefs and negative emotions, you can begin to reprogram your subconscious mind. It can actually be very simple. There are many techniques that you can learn and read about, such as repeating affirmations, practicing meditation, emotional freedom technique (EFT), and more.

> **TIP 3:** There are ways to clear limiting beliefs and negative emotions without much effort (such as listening to an mp3 or wearing a glyph). Visit https://choosamazing.com for free ideas on how to do this.

When you have removed any limiting beliefs and negative feelings about your goals, you can start the actual manifesting process with the Law of Attraction.

2. SET INTENTIONS AND BE SPECIFIC

Decide exactly what you want to manifest. Set an intention. Make sure to answer these important questions: What? When? Why? How? (What specifically do you want? Why do you want it? How will it benefit you and others?). If you are not specific, you might get random results or worse yet, confuse the universe and not get any results.

For example, let's say that you decide that your intention is to manifest a new car. Now be specific. What model is it? What color? How much do you want to pay for it? Describe the car in detail and list all of its features. You can't attract something that isn't specified. It would be like going to a car dealership and saying that you want to buy a car without providing any other information. There are so many types of cars with so many different features. You have to pick something specific: color, price, size, etc. The same principle applies when you are using the Law of Attraction to manifest anything. Make sure to also answer "why you want this" and "what benefit it will bring you and others." **It is also useful to know that you might get what you specified "or something better" because it might not show up exactly the way you specified it, but could be even better!**

> **TIP:** Do your research carefully. Do you want a specific thing? Research its characteristics, price, size, color, etc. Find out your preferred type, brand, its features and anything else that could be helpful in getting what you desire.

Knowing the specifics of what you want to manifest will also help you with the next step of visualizing your goal. You can write this in your Law of Attraction planner or journal if you use one.

> IMPORTANT: Please note that your level of desire is crucial! On a scale of 1-10, with 10 being the highest, how much do you actually desire the object or outcome that you are trying to manifest? Make sure that you know your level of desire before you start attracting anything into your life.

3. **VISUALIZE AND BELIEVE**

In order to attract something, you have to BELIEVE that you can have it. When it comes to manifesting your dream, your level of belief determines the outcome. If you don't believe it, you won't get it. Are you trying to manifest winning the lottery? Do you believe that it's actually possible? Do you want a new car? Do you believe that you can have it? It is important that you visualize and believe that you ALREADY HAVE what you are interested in manifesting with the Law of Attraction. On a scale of 1-10, 10 being the highest, how much do you actually believe that you can have what you want? If you're waiting for a manifestation miracle, it won't happen if you don't believe that it is possible.

If you have the feeling of WANT, that communicates to the universe that you are actually LACKING what you need, and so you won't get your request. You have to substitute the feeling of "want" with that of "I already have it." This is key in manifesting your desires.

There is a sweet spot for making the Law of Attraction work for you. The secret on how to manifest what you want quickly in your life is to hit the sweet spot. This means having a heartfelt desire (which is different than a lacking "want") and a strong belief in the possibility of having what you are attracting.

> IMPORTANT: Following your joy and being in the heart, as described earlier, can also help you manifest your desires faster. When you are in your heart, you physically change your reality because of the electromagnetic field of the heart.

> **TIP 1:** A very important step in manifesting what you want is to visualize your goal while having positive feelings (some people

say to visualize for 68 seconds, but you can do it for a longer time if you like). Imagine yourself ALREADY HAVING what you would like to manifest and feel extremely joyful about it. Visualize this for as long as you want. You can't get distracted during this time. Your thought needs to be focused, clear and pure.

******Focus is very important because energy goes where your attention is.***

For example, imagine that you are in your dream car right now. What does it feel like? What does it smell like? What music is on the radio? Involve all of your senses (see, touch, smell, taste, hear) and BELIEVE this is actually happening and that you ALREADY HAVE it.

Using your senses creates a complete picture and makes the experience more real. Imagine the scenario just like you did when you were a child and played a pretend game. Think, how would a kid visualize this situation? What would they do to make it seem more real? How did you make things seem real when you were little? Use those strategies to visualize and believe that you already have what you want and are already experiencing what you would like to manifest.

TIP 2: If you are looking to manifest an item, try the following exercise. Go on a website that you are interested in shopping on, start adding to your shopping cart everything that you would like to buy. You don't have to actually buy the products. You are just adding them to your cart as if you are really shopping. This is a great exercise to strengthen your belief that what you want is actually happening. When you see your items in the shopping cart, it's easier to imagine that you ALREADY HAVE them.

TIP 3: Get excited about what you are visualizing! Feel happy when you think about it. Believe that you deserve it.

TIP 4: Imagine that other people also receive what you manifested. Some experts state that when you visualize others having the same thing as your wish, the power of the manifestation gets amplified and you attract it more easily and faster. So let's say you want to manifest $3000. Imagine your friends also receiving $3000, everyone in your city receiving $3000, etc. Feel excited about everyone getting the amount of money that you manifested for yourself.

TIP 5: If you are still having trouble believing, you can try the "wouldn't it be nice if" exercise. This simply means that you form statements using "what if" or "wouldn't it be nice if." For example, you can say "Wouldn't it be nice if I had a new house?" or "Wouldn't it be nice if I had a new car?" This should make it easier for you to imagine the scenario and visualize what that experience would be like.

TIP 6: Write out in a Law of Attraction journal how you are visualizing your manifested goal. When you write, you get your mind more focused. Instead of spending a few seconds visualizing, writing ideas takes longer and your mind will be engaged for a longer period.

If you are still having trouble visualizing and believing, then go back to the beginning and work on removing your limiting beliefs.

4. FEEL POSITIVE EMOTIONS: LOVE AND GRATITUDE

Everything is energy. How you feel determines what you attract. When you experience an emotion, your body gives off a certain energetic vibration. You match a specific "frequency." This is where the Law of Vibration comes in. It's important to connect emotionally to what you intend to manifest. Feeling love and gratitude raises your vibration. These are two of the most powerful emotions that you can experience.

Think of this like a radio. You can't listen to the radio station that you want if you are not on the right channel! It's absolutely necessary that you tune your signal to the right frequency. **You have to match the frequency of what you are trying to manifest.**

> **TIP 1:** Feel love for yourself to attract a significant other. Feel love for money if you intend to manifest wealth. Feel love for a car if that's what you would like to attract, etc. If feeling love for an object sounds weird to you, then you can try feeling gratitude for having it instead.

Feel grateful that you ALREADY HAVE what you want. Think that you already manifested it, that you LOVE it and be THANKFUL for this. Also, be grateful for what you currently have in your life. So for example, if you are trying to manifest more money, be grateful for the money that you have right now. You have to actually FEEL grateful. You can't just say that you are if you don't believe it/ feel it.

TIP 2: Take a walk in nature and notice how different your energy feels. Nature can help you vibrate at a higher frequency, which is what you need in order to be able to manifest good things into your life. Once you are in a park or some other location where you can connect with nature, try adding the feelings of love and gratitude and notice how much better you feel. This is a powerful formula for raising your vibration. Once you are in this high vibrational state, start visualizing your goal as mentioned in step 3 above.

TIP 3: List what you are grateful for in present tense. Make it a daily habit before you go to sleep and right after you wake up to think, say, or write at least 5 things that you are grateful for. This gets you in the habit of feeling good and grateful.

TIP 4: Think about what manifesting your goal would bring you. How would it make your life better? What would it allow you to do? Again, think in present tense, not future. What would be happening right now? For example, why do you want more money? You could say that you want more money because it allows you to travel to exotic islands. Now imagine what it would be like to relax there right now. Focus on the effect that attracting money would have. It's also useful to think about sharing the money that you get with others. What people would you give money to? What charities would you donate to?

Thinking in these terms can raise your vibration. This is also helpful if you have limiting beliefs because by focusing on the effect that your manifested goal would have, you are not directly focusing on your goal. So if you are working on manifesting abundance and have a limiting belief about money, but you don't have a limiting belief about traveling, then thinking about all of the traveling that you would do with the money that you manifest should make it easier to use the Law of Attraction.

You have to stay in a high vibration when it comes to attracting your goal, which means thinking good thoughts and feeling positive emotions. Otherwise, you will be distancing yourself from what you are trying to manifest.

> **Remember, high vibration (feeling good and happy) = positive experiences; Low vibration (feeling bad) = negative experiences.**

No matter how you feel throughout the day, you should try to always feel good and excited about the goal that you would like to manifest. If you have a tendency to be negative or get in a bad mood, you can create positive daily reminders to transform low vibrational energy and bring you back to a high vibration. These are reminders throughout your day that help you feel good about what you are manifesting.

Try to stay aware of your mood and feelings during the day and as soon as you notice that you are getting off track, bring yourself back to feeling good and thinking positive thoughts. So even if you get in a bad mood about something, you can quickly remind yourself to get back on the positive side.

> **TIP 5:** You can set an alarm on your phone that goes off a few times a day and reminds you to become aware of how you feel in that moment. Replace any negative thoughts with positive ones. Get excited about your goal and think happy thoughts about it as if you already have it (for example, you can say to yourself "I love my new car!" You can also post notes around your house that include a happy phrase related to your goal, so every time you look at it, you will be reminded to stay positive. This helps with your beliefs and keeping your vibration high.

5. EXPECT TO GET IT AND LET GO

After completing the steps above, just let go and wait for your desire to manifest. Don't check if it's happening and don't ask how it will happen. However, you can visualize what you are trying to manifest every day or a few times a week, if that resonates with you (don't check if it's happening, just visualize and feel as if you already have it).

You don't have to know HOW it will happen. Just trust the process and believe that it will arrive soon (but you have to actually believe it, otherwise you'll just be wasting your time). Don't be impatient or anxious. If you NEED it (if you are feeling lack) you won't get it. Expect to get it. Trust that it's coming.

This last step of letting go is very important in learning how to manifest anything you want. If you're constantly asking "where is it?" that means you have doubts and/or are impatient, which creates negative feelings and distances you from your goal. So let go and just relax. Let things happen when the time is right and when your energy is aligned with what you are trying to manifest. Then comes the step of taking inspired action when you get an idea of something that you would feel good doing.

6. TAKE INSPIRED ACTION

It may seem strange, but you have to "prove" to the universe that you are serious about what you are trying to manifest. Take inspired action when you feel the desire to do something that will bring you closer to your goal. Don't force things. Tune into your intuition and feelings and see if you sense what actions you might take. They should make you feel good and positive.

> **TIP:** Here is an example of inspired action. Let's say that you are trying to manifest a new phone. One day you randomly get an urge to take a walk. You wonder what to do. Well, you probably should take that walk. You would be surprised at the cool synchronicities that the Law of Attraction can bring you. When going on that walk you might meet a friend who might tell you about a great sale where you can get an amazing discount on a phone or even a free one! Anything is possible. Take positive actions that open you to possibilities.

Taking inspired action is an important step. You can't just sit around and wait. Act "as if" you already have manifested what you want. What would you be doing right now?

Please remember to examine your limiting beliefs before taking any action because if your subconscious mind rejects what you are trying to manifest, then you probably won't have success with the Law of Attraction.

7. **BE GRATEFUL AND CELEBRATE**

To experience the awesomeness of the Law of Attraction, start by manifesting something small in order to build your belief and train your subconscious mind. When you get it, celebrate your results. Be GRATEFUL. The more grateful you are, the more you will get of what you are grateful for. Say to yourself "How much better can things get?" and "What other amazing things are waiting for me today?"

> IMPORTANT: If for some reason you are not receiving what you tried to manifest, remember to work on your subconscious beliefs as discussed in step 1 of the manifesting process. It could also be that your soul and "Higher Self" want something better for you, so it is important to feel if what you desire is actually coming from your heart.

"Focus only on what you would like to experience."

@choosamazing

CONCLUSION

The planet and people are raising their vibration. We are becoming aware of many things about our reality that we weren't aware of before. The most powerful manifestation technique of all is being in the heart. Even science has shown that this can help you attract your dreams.

Your awareness, focus, frequency and vibration determine what you will experience each moment. **The way to manifest an amazing life easily and effortlessly is to stay in the heart (which enables you to have coherence and attract your heart's desires), do only what you want to do and follow your joy (which raises your vibration and allows more of what brings you joy to show up in your reality), remain aware and fully present in the moment (which lets you manifest your highest potential), focus only on that which you would like to experience (energy goes where you place your attention), and take inspired action.**

Creating an incredible reality has to do with changing your perception, raising your vibration, and expanding your consciousness. May you manifest your heart's desires easily, effortlessly, and joyfully!

If you enjoyed this book, visit https://choosamazing.com for more tips, ideas, and inspiration.

"You are the creator. Your life is your creation. Every moment is an opportunity to become aware of your creativity."

@choosamazing

GLOSSARY

3D (Third Dimension): Also known as third density, this is the dimension we have been living in. It has limitations, suffering, duality, negative emotions and low vibrations.

5D (Fifth Dimension): Also known as fourth density, this is a high frequency dimension that we are moving toward in the ascension/awakening process. It has to do with being fully present in the moment and living from the heart, which allows our energy to be coherent. In this dimension we experience peace, love, and joy and are free of suffering and judgment. We have a high vibration and experience higher frequencies.

11:11: This is an awakening code, an activation. It is related to the ascension/awakening process that we are in.

Ascension: People and the planet are raising their vibration and moving from the third dimension (3D) to the fifth dimension (5D)/fourth density. This involves being aware and in the heart, which makes your energy coherent and raises your vibration.

Coherence: This is a harmonious state. When your energy is coherent, it helps you to stay physically, mentally, and emotionally healthy. It allows you to experience your highest potential. Having heart and brain coherence is your superpower that changes reality.

Consciousness: It is awareness. This is what you really are. You are not your body. You are consciousness/awareness experiencing life through your physical body.

Duality: This is believing in good/bad, right/wrong, etc. This leads to judgment and suffering. The 3D dimension is one of duality.

Enlightenment: The simple definition of enlightenment is "being aware that you are aware." This means becoming aware of your awareness in the moment. The physical body also has to clear any low vibrational frequencies/emotions, so that it can raise its vibration. This can be done with energy work very easily by listening to energy clearing mp3s, using glyphs, meditation, or other techniques that help the body clear stuck energy/emotions. It's not true that only some people who meditate for years can become enlightened. We are already in the ascension/awakening process and ANYONE can become enlightened if they choose. Everyone can "become aware that they are aware." You don't need to meditate on a mountain for years to achieve this state.

Frequency: Energy vibrates at different rates. The frequency of something is the rate at which it vibrates.

Higher Self/Authentic Self: This is a high vibrational version of yourself that is always in joy and is free of judgment and duality. Your Higher Self is "guiding" you through your intuition, ideas, etc. When you follow your joy, you are listening to your Higher Self.

Law of Attraction: This universal law focuses on the idea that like attracts like. Positive thoughts, beliefs and emotions attract positive experiences and negative thoughts, beliefs, and emotions attract negative experiences.

Law of Vibration: This universal law explains that everything is always in motion and vibrates at a certain frequency. So what you attract into your life depends on your vibration and frequency.

Nonduality: This is the recognition of being one with everything and that there is only one indivisible reality underneath all of the diversity of objects, people, things, etc. Nonduality teaches that you are consciousness, which is infinite and eternal.

Self-Love: This means being fully present in the moment, being true to who you are, accepting yourself, not judging yourself, and forgiving yourself for everything.

The Awakening: This refers to waking up from the "illusion" (the 3D duality matrix) we have been living in. The awakening is helping us realize that we are not separate from each other and from the Divine/Source/Spirit/God, etc., and that there is more to this physical reality than what we have been told. It is helping us move to the fifth dimension (5D)/fourth density and discover that we are consciousness and the creators of our reality. It is the process of letting go of duality, raising our vibration, and moving to a higher dimension. It's also referred to as "ascension."

Vibration: This is the movement of energy.

ABOUT THE AUTHOR

Diana lived in four countries and traveled around the world, which led her on a spiritual journey to realize that there is more to this physical reality. She worked in marketing for some of the biggest corporations in the U.S. and Europe before having a spiritual awakening and starting her own company to help people discover and choose the amazing things in life. She is exploring and sharing simple and effective techniques that raise one's vibration and expand their consciousness.

Printed in the USA
CPSIA information can be obtained
at www.ICGtesting.com
CBHW071815290324
6072CB00015B/1439

9 781088 220108